Meals Around the World

Meals in Russia

by R.J. Bailey

Bullfrog Books

Ideas for Parents and Teachers

Bullfrog Books let children practice reading informational text at the earliest reading levels. Repetition, familiar words, and photo labels support early readers.

Before Reading

- Discuss the cover photo. What does it tell them?

- Look at the picture glossary together. Read and discuss the words.

Read the Book

- "Walk" through the book and look at the photos. Let the child ask questions. Point out the photo labels.

- Read the book to the child, or have him or her read independently.

After Reading

- Prompt the child to think more. Ask: Have you ever eaten Russian food? Were the flavors new to you? What did you like best?

Bullfrog Books are published by Jump!
5357 Penn Avenue South
Minneapolis, MN 55419
www.jumplibrary.com

Library of Congress Cataloging-in-Publication Data

Names: Bailey, R.J., author.
Title: Meals in Russia / by R.J. Bailey.
Description: Minneapolis, MN: Jump!, Inc. [2017]
Series: Meals around the world | Audience: Ages 5–8.
Audience: K to grade 3. | Includes index.
Identifiers: LCCN 2016014990 (print)
LCCN 2016015810 (ebook)
ISBN 9781620313763 (hardcover: alk. paper)
ISBN 9781620314944 (pbk.)
ISBN 9781624964237 (ebook)
Subjects: LCSH: Food—Russia—Juvenile literature.
Cooking, Russian—Juvenile literature.
Food habits—Russia—Juvenile literature.
Classification: LCC TX723.3 .B34 2017 (print)
LCC TX723.3 (ebook) | DDC 394.1/20947--dc23
LC record available at https://lccn.loc.gov/2016014990

Editor: Jenny Fretland VanVoorst
Series Designer: Ellen Huber
Book Designer: Leah Sanders
Photo Researcher: Leah Sanders

Photo Credits: All photos by Shutterstock except:
Alamy, 15; Corbis, 8.

Printed in the United States of America at Corporate Graphics in North Mankato, Minnesota.

Table of Contents

Pancake Week

Wake up! It is pancake week.

We eat blini.
We drink hot tea.

5

Boris likes warm kasha.

He eats it every morning.

We dress up.

We go to the festival.

What does Olga buy?
A stack of blini. Yum!

In Russia, lunch
is the big meal.

Papa grills shashlik.

It smells good.

Klara eats borscht.
It is a beet soup.
She has it with
dark bread.

13

It is time for dinner.

Mama makes pelmeni.

**They are little dumplings.
What is inside? Meat.**

fish eggs ·····▶

We eat fish.

Ivan likes fish eggs.

He puts them on blini!

What is for dessert?
Cheese pancakes.

We can eat more
pancakes tomorrow!

Make Blini!

Make Russian pancakes! Be sure to get an adult to help.

Ingredients:

- 2 eggs
- 1 tablespoon white sugar
- ½ teaspoon salt
- ½ cup all-purpose flour
- 2½ cups milk
- 1 tablespoon vegetable oil
- 1 tablespoon butter

Directions:

❶ In a medium bowl, whisk the eggs, sugar, and salt.

❷ Sift the flour into the bowl. Stir in the milk.
   Mix until the batter is thin.

❸ Heat a griddle over medium heat. Lightly oil the griddle.

❹ Pour 2 tablespoons of batter into the pan. Tilt the pan
   to spread the batter.

❺ When the edges look crisp and the center looks dry,
   slide a spatula under the blini.

❻ Flip and cook on the other side until lightly browned.

❼ Put blini on a plate. Stack the blini on top of each other.
   Put the butter on top.

❽ Take a blini. Spread with jam and fold in half two times
   to make a triangle. Enjoy!

Picture Glossary

blini
A thin pancake.

pancake week
A Russian festival that celebrates the transition of winter into spring.

borscht
A hot or cold soup made with red beets, which are a root vegetable.

pelmeni
Small dumplings filled with chopped meat.

kasha
A grain cereal usually made from buckwheat.

shashlik
Grilled or cooked meat on a stick.

23

Index

To Learn More

Learning more is as easy as 1, 2, 3.

1) Go to www.factsurfer.com

2) Enter "mealsinRussia" into the search box.

3) Click the "Surf" button to see a list of websites.

With factsurfer.com, finding more information is just a click away.